THE SHANGHAI OWNER
OF THE
BONSAI SHOP

HILARY DAVIES

The Shanghai Owner
of the
Bonsai Shop

LONDON
ENITHARMON PRESS
1991

First published in 1991
by the Enitharmon Press
BCM Enitharmon
London WC1N 3XX

Distributed in the USA
by Dufour Editions Inc.
PO Box 449, Chester Springs
Pennsylvania 19425

ISBN 1 870612 56 6 (paper)
ISBN 1 870612 86 8 (cloth)

The paperback edition is limited to 800 copies
and the cloth edition to 25 signed and numbered copies

Set in 10pt Ehrhardt by Bryan Williamson, Darwen
and printed by
Billing & Sons Ltd, Worcester

ACKNOWLEDGEMENTS

Some of these poems have appeared in: *Agenda, Encounter, Entailles* (France), the *Eric Gregory Anthology 1983-4, Exile* (Canada), *The Honest Ulsterman, New Poetry 5, Orbis, The Phoenix Review* (Australia), *Poetry Book Society Anthology 1988, Poésie Europe, Poetry Wales, Quarry* (Canada), *The Rialto, The Times Literary Supplement, 2 Plus 2* (Switzerland), *Verse, Writing Women, The Orange Dove of Fiji* (World Wildlife Poetry Anthology) 1989.

'Fulbeck, 1944' was broadcast on BBC Radio 3's 'Poetry Now' in 1984.

'Dead in Vienna' won 2nd prize in the Cardiff Festival Poetry Competition in 1986.

'The Ophthalmologist' won 1st prize in the Times Literary Supplement/Cheltenham Literature Festival Poetry Competition in 1987.

'So I Climbed Out of the Hatch' won joint 3rd prize in the Leek Festival Poetry Competition in 1989.

Some of these poems formed part of a collection which received an Eric Gregory Award for poets under 30 from the Society of Authors in 1983.

David Hockney's *Rain on the Terrace, Los Angeles* (colour photograph, 1980) is reproduced by kind permission of the artist.

Contents

for Bill
who saw it through

I

IN THE DYING LIGHT OF A DAY NOT ENTERED

In the Dying Light of a Day Not Entered

In the dying light of a day not entered
Stepped out into the straight street's grid.
Found air touching, very gently, rooftops, windows,
Fingering a leaf and moving on then to the balustrades
Of children looping with thin voices
The whole city. Felt the squat and tall
Spires turning with fastidiousness
As parents move and talk around their child asleep.
And all the buildings of the place had grown this distance,
Vanguard against the break of afternoon to evening:
Without, the towers will topple and the river rut.

When dark comes the city lets its breath go
Out of the reddened doors and halls of night,
But the child in bed at the top of the house
Voyages elsewhere,
Cresting on what wide light was here, what pastel seas.

The Ophthalmologist

We are in a very dark room.
He has the air of one not gone above
For years; his whisper shows
He is completely in command down here.
So I commend myself into his gentle fingers
That play around my head more intimately
Than most men's should do, the trembling
At my ear, the pressure on my temples,
Making me turn profile from side to side,
The touch testing my neck.
He has many categories of sight, ranged
In little boxes, a long, a short, an astigmatism
In a prism of glass. His machinery
Flickers an instant before me, lenses
You'd love to turn in your hand
Like ovals of limestone, waxy as opal.
All the kingdoms he shows me of letters
From their different angles: bold,
Crabbed, melancholic. I peer through
The thicknesses, pitting myself guiltily
Against deft fingers, the deferential mask.

Half an hour's enough to pinpoint all my weaknesses;
How to correct blur, squint, failure to see things
As they really are. I've grown to like
The shadowiness with which we work,
How outlines turn to sculpture, the world
Dividing into lamplight and the dark.
When he throws wide the door, I cannot rise
Towards the greening surface;
Under the desks and curtains the eye-doctor
Offers the lure of many visions,
The honey of his systems underground.

The Magnolia

She sits, winding the slow coil of her thoughts:
Wire into the brain.
From this place she would hear the bells sing across the town
And young men's voices on summer afternoons
Far off from the sanded walks below,
As they went to tea, or bicycled, or were just going shopping
For something in town:
Won't be long.

Words guarantors of their return,
Of ritual appointments they would keep,
The sanctity of tea, cricket, dinner
And evenings chosen to be alone,
No tearing at the mind, or time.

Here, rested in her chrysalis-bier,
She listened once to their world of movement,
Muffled stirring of a country on the other side,
Uncared for, not needed
In her kingdom's dark oyster shell:
No power on earth to make it break before the flood.

Long past the clock had ceased counting the hours –
Never, though she had watched, afraid,
Had its face known change.
Books, chintz window seat, the wide-brimmed hat upon the wall
She wove into her love's fable,
Herself into a ravelled skein of dreams.

Now, as she curls, she sees still the chapel buttresses
Push straightway to heaven,
Massively rooting their great wings in earth;
Here, amid the season's first flowering,
A magnolia grows, twists on itself,
Squanders its life and bloom in new birth,
Sap running through the wound into beauty:
Silken petals on the grass.

Their blasting has split wide the chrysalis,
Broken her shell, and the shell of the tree's flowers,
What no hand, no sickness nor voyage could do.
The clock strikes; her lover will not come –
She opens now to time, the sun's changing,
Moth stilled for ever in its fragile womb.

Camogli

This postcard's a sealed bottle,
Over ten years to deliver the message
I started reading that afternoon
When the light was like knives
And the sea stained me with its salt
Blisters. And I gathered up my book
And walked out of the sun and the shouting
Tourists, under the eaves of the oozing houses.
The women hung like black sails anticipating
Their own bereavement coming
Over the horizon, ready to throw themselves down
Into the clemency of Our Lady of the Sea
As I walked up the church steps
Dripped on by gutters and run around by dogs.

And, though I read, or tried to read,
All that afternoon into the complexities
And hideous dark of men's souls,
All I remember is the endless shuffling
Of sacristan and old lady, the stone
As exquisitely cold as a lover's blade going in,
And a world of children crying and calling
At the edge of the ocean far below me,
Calling and calling forever as they go
Wading into the Pity of Our Lady of Time
Who holds us all in the sweet
Dazzle of her hand.

Each Day the Chignonned Women Gather

Each day the chignonned women gather
On the train; their skin is drawn so tight
The veins pulse blue as painter's ink
Tracing fragility. They bend their heads together
Like birds and then revert to stillness.
Around them, the other travellers make space,
Raising occasionally a languid eye whose look
Founders on their cool bones and passes on.
They carry, without heeding, balance
Into other halls that we know nothing of
And spend themselves till evening on exercises
To lend and learn grace. They should be inviolate:
Their faces are like china – a leaf, a cherry blossom
Would break them. They chatter unknowingly
While all around the underworld grows greater
Planning how he will win such delicacy
To his desires.

Sunflower

We had no business to pick this flower
But you said what did it matter
Seeing there were so many, better
Than being pressed into oil for cooking;
And indeed they had been waving
Along our path all day, straining
And turning after their own image,
All in different stages of growth and ripening.
Till in the end you wanted to know
What lay at the centre, how the heat
Pushed out into the dazzling petals,
Why the core turned black. Now I watch
Astonished how this fruit spreads itself spikily
Across the dashboard, elbowing us out
With its high-pitched 'yallow, yallow'
Like a king's fool. You drive me past churches,
Citadels, cornfields, happy with the company
Of this big sun pod that looks jovially at us
Out of the windscreen.

It's only when we seek rest at evening
We discover how we've been bewitched
By this outrageous cinder: beside our bed
All night long he keeps nodding and dancing,
Wrapping his warm yellow drapes
Around us as we make love.

Landing at Dubai

So we have landed here:
Our vessel creeps along the shore,
Unwinged, coasting
With all the weariness of the inanimate bird.
We are also weary; there is no laughter,
Only the sound and movement of many families
Who like sleepwalkers gather up their luggage
And sway in the aisles like trees in unison.
We have been inside, hours over water;
The slow gestures of the travellers reach us,
Before drowning in the outside air.

We too are poised to step indifferently down into the darkness
Where desert ferries shuttle like ants beneath monstrous heels.
Everything is anticipated: how we must wait
And crowd, dream fitful dreams upon anonymous chairs,
Slung between where we have come from
And where we are going to.

But nothing in what we encounter
Is what we have envisaged it to be:
The moon's a succulent, big fruit on the horizon
The desert opens like a nectarine,
And inexplicably the scent of water
Comes from under stones we know do not feel rain.

There's no intemperance here
Except in the meagreness of our imaginings
That only find in this exhausted place
A wilderness, and not the rounded pomander
It is. We are already giddy as we touch the ground
And look about us. A distant flare
Flowers at the sea's edge where what lies underground
Bursts to the surface and irradiates the air.

'Forty Days Adrift in an Open Boat'

'Forty days adrift in an open boat:
It was good, the clean cut of the sea,
Its indifference not to be thought hostility
Under the burning sun. On the third day
The tunnies came, nudging at fingers and legs,
And I felt closer, going down
Into the dark bubble of water. Each day
The relinquishing of a new thing:
First desire, then hunger, till I lay
Like a stick in the boat.

This continued for seven days before the compass broke
And my harpoon punctured the dinghy's side.
I realised the jostling was greater
And the jaws aiming for vulnerable features
Especially at night when I lit the flares
Or burned my lamp, very low, for company.
Soon something inside me gave,
And the blood of the first tuna
And his mate thrashing at me, the murderer,
Kept me awake. Whether they sought
To turn me to prey or because they saw
Through their glassy ceiling how lonely
The voyage was, they never left me.

In the morning light, I would recognise
The scars and scratches of one biggish female
Who led the troupe, the livid marks
Of love and aggression streaking down her back
As she pushed with her acolytes forward.
Beside me always the pink, inflamed eye
Of the widow waiting for me to move too incautiously
Sideways, though she herself not so prudent,
Several times slashed with my bow
And bleeding as we entered warmer waters.

One afternoon, after sleep and rising thirsty
To the leaking vessel of water, I saw,
Standing over me almost, a sail boat
And three black fishermen staring
At more tunny than they had ever seen.
A hesitation, then I beckoned them forward,
Showed them my outriders, my fish ambassadors
To a newfoundland. Suddenly, swift, all around me
The joyous heave, pitch, thrust of the heavy fish
From the ocean, my tried confederates
Banged in a welter of guts and lashing
Onto the frail decks; and I, though starving
And having suffered much, lay at peace
In the bottom of the boat, and listened
To the incredulous shouting of fishermen
Taking their harvest out of the hissing sea.'

Lemur

I came here first.
I had to myself the savannah
And the dark of the rain forest.
I ate the fruits at my ease
And picked the dew out of the flowers'
Cusp. I copulated
With my own kind, until each suited
Bush, or lolloping over
The ground, or watching everything
From the summit of the trees.
We grew fur all colours of the rainbow,
Hands more delicate than cobwebs,
Ears that could hear a grub
Crawling underground. Around us
Lifted the fortress of the immaculate sea.

I have grown cunning since then.
Our eyes perfected to see clearer
All things dark, the black
Moving at the heart of things.
We hide in the treetrunks at noonday,
Drop like stones out of the twilight.
My teeth have grown too large,
Show always through my lips like
A jaw decomposing. The new inhabitants
Fear my third digit: when I hear them
Coming like innocents through the undergrowth,
I crook my long finger to the one
I will favour, watch with my vast
And incurious eyes his companions
Lay out his incandescent white bones.

So I Climbed Out of the Hatch

So I climbed out of the hatch
Following the order that had come
From deep within the ship
To try the rigging. Began to step
Up and along the ropes, testing
And pulling my weight against the wind
Bitter and from the north. Salt
Flayed my eyes and hands till I
Could feel and see and think of
No more but the next strong twist
Of creosoted line my life was strung on.
But then came one from the belly
Of the ship behind me, with whom I'd
Eaten, drunk, and shared a bed,
Lifting his gentle eyes up.
Called encouragement against the tossing
And started out along the spar
As my safeguard, his voice as powerful
As the rope that bore us.
Yet I, too conscious of my weakness,
Clinging with all my sinew
To the cordage, moved on by inches
Not looking down nor up, but only
Concentrating on the texture of this
One grip, this moment in my hand.
And now I do not know how many years
Have slipped away since first I started
Up into the storm, but notice
How powerful I am become, and ruthless,
Finding myself wide out along this spar
And catching far far below me his desperate voice,
His dying gentle eyes.

In the Hollow Bud of Nature

In the hollow bud of nature,
Grows within something
Self-sufficient, determinate,
Another core less certain to the eye
Or touch, a filament, a tiny spore
Sending out threaders. So,
While the living thing feeds,
And sucks along the branch,
The itch begins. At first
Grows in the feelers, the outward
Reaching to drops of water, light,
Heat, recognition. Then the slow
Running down through all the organism
Until all urges guide it one way only,
Away from company, the solace of its kind,
Into a rare forest. This first the time
The beast starts to run sick,
Turn out of kilter where it should pursue
The ordinary course of matter: eyes
Bulge with visions, the mind grown
Elephantine with its parasite.
See here the end result: this waifthread
Simulacrum of a body, enmeshed
As if remetamorphosed back to nothing:
While from its skull creeps Poetry
With fangs unfurled.

II

THE PRISONER OF KATYN

The Tower

His childhood was spent in a tower
And he always found it normal how small
The people were, how slowly they moved
Except when his father heaved on the bell
Under the eavings; then they gathered up
Their skirts or animals and scattered
Before the luminous red line in the forest.
The stairs at the end of the room went down
Deep and wide to the uncertain earth
And from them his father erupted at nightfall
With stories to make his head swim:
Of fools at crossroads, two-headed calves,
How simple Anna was found in Bratislava
And wouldn't tell with whom she had been.
Only the fiddler came from below,
Threading the town's staccato cries,
Deaths, wooing, through the bow's strait eye.
So fine an ear he could eventually hear
Each bug rustle in the skirting,
The ants congregate beneath the window sill
For the fiddle's story. When he placed
His ear to the eddying ground long after
He heard sound through the city's crackle
That lullabying, the ceaseless scything
Of a cricket's thin elegy, the lovers' undersong.

The Ballad of Limehouse Reach

They lay not far from the mudflats
In a dark, half-way house:
He had come from a tea-clipper
And she from a drunken spouse

He led her up the stairway
Smelling of tar and wine
She did not look to right or left
And no light shone

He opened the door of the attic
Where no fire was set
But the fire of his arms as he took her
And his hair shimmered jet

He slept on her breast in the moonlight
His limbs were like a girl's
His skin was fine as satin
And he wore a ring of pearls

His skin was smooth as satin
In the winter air
When the sun rose up that morning
Pearls of frost were in his hair

'Where will you go?' she asked him
'Upon what foreign seas?
What new lands will you plunder
And sail with what warm breeze?'

'I'll sail across vast oceans
I'll sail to my home land
I'll dive among pearlfishers
And sleep upon the sand.

But when the shores are misty
And the tide is green
I'll think of fire in winter
And of a pale woman dream.'

He led her down the stairway
He kissed her on the quay
She saw him mount the gangplank
She saw the sails run free

Now when she lies near the mudflats
And hears the ships come home
She lights a candle in the window
In her hair she puts a comb

And though there's no-one climbs it
There's a creak upon the stair
She turns a pair of white hands
To touch the jet-black hair

'For his eyes were dark as sloefruit
And his limbs were like a girl's
His skin was soft as satin
And he had a ring of pearls.'

Night Story

The woman holding her friend
Up the six flights to bed is wound
In a new wind which all day in the drunk man's head
Has hidden where he could not reach
Or know exactly when it would breach their polite exteriors.
The sky tight across a setting city
Will not absolve them, nor the men sleeping
Who rise angrily and couch them without tenderness
Like sacks among tears and glasses,
And then lie indifferent to the metaphysic
And prayer urged in a foreign language
Through the night air by him
Who tomorrow will shave and eat
And deny there was anything ever said here.

Freydis Meets the Skraelings

*(Skraeling was the name given by the Vikings to the
inhabitants of Vinland and Greenland)*

She had been tending the fire,
Didn't notice the whirr
Of the anti-clockwise sticks,
The setting up of the pale blue
Ballista on the pole. She was stirring
Ashes, mindful of weight in her belly,
Shifting her feet to get more comfort,
Running her fingers over the swell
Which would be her first-born.

So when the cries came to her
As from a great distance,
She imagined them hauling
A whale up the beach, thought
Of how fat would spit in the hearth,
How she would cut slabs like
Red butter. Then past her window
Went husband and brother
Without a glance, running into
The wood. And Freydis stood
At her threshold, did as her mother
Had told her, laughed at their
White flashing legs, their
Scattered weapons.

The child made her heavy as a cow.
At the clearing she turned, knowing
She was done for. Freydis,
Under the cool maples, pulled
From her dead men a sword,
Watched the Skraelings show
Their broad cheeks, their woad.
Out from her undershirt lifted
A breast traced with blue,
Miraculous. Grisly; with the sword
Slapped loudly upon it, flack, flack,
The blade sheer and lovely in the sun.

Tonight the men load the beams
Of her house with fish:
Freydis has wrapped their swords
In blankets, tells and retells
How she met the Skraelings in the forest.
The trees keep vigil outside their compound,
Ask each other over and over,
Where will you drop
Your first-born, woman with breasts
White as bison fat, sword goddess,
Stinking shaman, conjuring ships
With wolves' heads onto our hishing sands?

Dominikus Zimmermann

Like a barn: he said, the externals do not matter
Though upon the exact date of this learning
There was no consensus. Certainly not from father,
Uncle or brother. At nine years in Josephus' workshop
Watched the men bevel till from silence
They drew a mad dog, a Virgin with Butterfly.
In the afternoon he saw the carpenters
Rounded against the open door like moons,
Their cloth backs flickering at dusk in the beer gardens.
At seventeen uncovered Emilie's thighs and found them white
As doves in storybooks
And when he worked the altar in the parish church
Gypsum and flesh performed the same undulations.
The fields of Wessobrunn were opal all that summer.

He took apprenticeship and saw a little of the wide river
And how magically its blue reflected heaven.
Noted for the first time the movement of a thing
From source to finish, though seeing neither,
Only the parable of what lay between.
That was enough. Then marriage. When they brought him
To the birthroom, sheets were streaked with blood
Like ancient lintels; downstairs,
A calf to celebrate the coming of a son.
When work resumed, he told the assistant builder
To place the cherubs upon draperies of pain,
The purgatory in red.

Easy at the end to accept the abbot's invitation,
Many things having reached their end, and little desire
For the stifled streets of Landsperg. The meadows reminded him
Of his mother fetching in the cows and mushrooms deliquescent after
     dawn.
It should be like a barn; the inner space provide
A case for nature, the white, blue, red
And upward thrust. His hand to cast
Petal and flagellation so finally to say
Between air, wood and interstices what he had learnt.

Then stay ten years to worship at his shrine
Walking each day from hut to organ loft
Under the cornice 'Dominikus Zimmermann',
Baumeister, carpenter, master builder.

Winchester Diver

Twenty-pound boots to keep him
Under the surface. Each morning
A dresser to weigh this leaf
Of bone down beneath the suspended
Cathedral; twelve men to pay out
The line and listen for the tug
And flow of his heart.

He works in utter dark, letting
The rivers in. They burst
From gravel beds and set
Logs that once were forests
Dappling the banks adrift into
His arms. Around him
Whisper the dreams of the
Casketed dead.

Pick, pick, pick with his hammer
And greased, bare hands.
His fingernails are black
With the ark's foundations;
She grinds and dances
On her shifting rock;
Wounds wide as hands
Open her flesh.

Down here the world's still
At its dead centre.
Stacking and slashing of cement
Turns the diver's ocean of
Salt to stone.
He'll beat out the fishes
Of his mind, stops up his ears
When tremors from the trench below
Burst their hearts. *Only*
Make this house safe, think of
Nothing but the work in hand.

And the queen and king are sailing
Home from the windless sea of Marmora;
Two owls that refuse escape are
Grouted in. Now the scaffolding
Rises into the free air away
From nightmares of whales,
Only children in violent reds
And whites, crowds shouting:
William Walker in his perfect
Dark shores up God's kingdom
On his back.

In Aphrodisias

No-one can bear to stand in the sun too long:
The men prefer to work in a more remote section,
Less promising, but away from the glare.
They sweat and carry big gourds of water,
They eat olives and bread lazily at noon
And throw stones at the frogs.

                           Then one,
One afternoon, runs to the foreman
Shouting 'Come, we're lifting her! Aphrodite!
It's taken twelve men.' The big face turns slowly
Uncovering her smile as the expert fingers
Brush dust away, and the workmen splay
Broad palms across neck and forehead,
Show their changed hands, laugh, and wipe
The glittering sand down blackened breeches.

'Raise her now gently'; and indifferently they weigh
Her body against their own, test hip, breast, thigh,
And delicately shift her on the pedestal
Until she pivots upright.
Then, shouting and joking under a wide evening sky,
They run past pools and colonnades to bicycles;
Behind the austere cypress a thin call to prayer
Shrills before shadows hide the goddess
With her plaited hair and impassive eyes:
Weaving home, the men dream
Of big-fleshed women, their waiting, silent wives.

Bacchus and Ariadne

He leaps: he is already lost.
These limbs will come jarring down
In front of his heedless gang,
The little satyr trailing blood
Out of an ass's throat.
Out of the now still cart,
Until this instant as swift as cheetahs,
Bacchus leaps into that diadem moment
Hung between the branches of time
And forever.

His face is turned to Ariadne like a deer
Pierced. And as a rout of dogs
Understanding nothing but the thicket
And the smell of blood his followers
Come wrapped in their red-hot lusts,
Girdled with snakes. Now, now,
Their thighs cry; the nymph's cymbals
Beat yes.

But Ariadne struggles with the sky,
The fleeting boat; how she could wish
The harbour of this bright blue cloak
Tight about her, bringing deliverance upward
Into eternity.
                    A passing dream:
Unwinding from her breast the manacle
Of love, red as a stain, redder by far
Than the hot season's trees, meshes
Him to her, holds his leap in air,
An age of longing lifted
Upon her mind's awakening glance.

Still instant, advent of the god:
Beggar our past lives as you do here
Dionysos leaping from our own dark forests
Hang upon heaven, set desire
In your faultless diadem.

Heine in Paris

How vast this room to the one eye tracing
Its lines of exploration to the door
Outside which onions slice, a woman admonishes
Before clicking four flights down beside the graveyard,
(O, All Souls' Day, the widows flowering
Amongst the sepulchres, green lovers
Lying under the cool yews!)
Till her return now there will be not silence
But these structures with which daily he fills his room
And masters all its changes: blue for summer
When the light should be bright as sand grains;
Red in winter to gash the snows outside
With pathways where his wife will walk protected
From overhanging things.
Today the world he inhabits is russet
And he heaps the multi-coloured leaves
In all the corners till his eyelids glow
With his own sunset. Now the waiting is easy:
In the afternoon he accompanies the gardeners,
Raking and watering with their arms,
Carried to exhaustion in their backs and thighs,
And drunk with light. When they go home,
He is lifted like a feather up the stairs.

She comes only when the curtains are drawn;
Sees in his hand the ever thinner traceries of blood:
'All afternoon I held you under the yew trees
And knew nothing but your scent, the grass,
Over my whole body the climax of the sun.'

The Mushroom Gatherer

When the summer visitors come out here
They first notice him at market
His oilcloth covered with horns of plenty,
Horse mushrooms, good-to-eat chanterelles.
'Buy for a soup pot, a stew, winter pickling
And salting'; his hands are filthy
As dead men's fingers, he lines his baskets with moss.
By noon he's around the outhouses
Asking for eggs and pullets; he mews
And smiles to cajole the women.
The visitors are sceptical when girls tell
How he dances in fairy rings, how his moustache
Is pale from drinking mushroom beer.
Yet every summer there's one who hitches up
Her skirt and goes with him under the broad-leaved trees
Which are the habitat of some, or among
Rotting branch heads, or dried dung.
They cut sticks and spend days in the forest,
Splaying freckled toes, feeling for mounds
That'll show them the dark convolutions of truffles.
When she returns, everyone's amazed at her sorting
Of baskets the greenhorns bring her,
Only the shade of a smile as she tosses out
He who is most handsome, the destroying angel,
Crafty cap, phallus impudicus.

In the Boboli Gardens

A bitter day. Cats coughing
Under the bushes; satyrs icy
Beneath the sky's grey coat.
This is not Aphrodite's season
For conjuring – away on every side
Drag worn-out centaurs, hang-dog dryads.
Greece and Rome squat about
As unremarkable as tamed goats.

This pigeon here is like the rest of us:
A kind of vulgar thing, short-sighted, engrossed
In grass. He turns and turns about us
Happy with the old familiar stink
Of domesticity, the mothballed benches
Where we prop our lives. Nor is discerning,
Nor suspects the secretness of trees
Which he thinks are merely for roosting.

But just below the lip of sight,
Of life, waits a soft bag of bones:
These eyes have no mercy for the unprepared;
They speak only judgment and sentence will be swift
Coming over the horizon in a flash of claw
So silent we have merely time to lift our wings
Once, and then are carried into the bushes
Where hugger-mugger we will be undone.

'Dead in Vienna'

'Dead in Vienna': Uncle Otto whom they never knew,
Would never know now, nor how long
He had lain beside the table (Louis Quinze),
Whether the silk or the velvet dressing-gown
To hide the stomach, which brush
To slick the hair over baldness,
How manicured the nails.
Nor how many weeks after the last person
Had climbed the shabby flights to his room
To suffer the uncertain talk, the pudgy hands,
Wanting it all to be over, and not to be touched,
But having to smile under the lamplight,
There being no alternative
If the escape from the even shabbier room
And the communal wash house was to endure,
And always the hope of something better,
As you smiled again, turned the head
In a slightly more appealing fashion
Sideways, thinking fast what compliment
For the flaccid man letting his watery eyes
Wander, offering cream, and later brandy
Before drawing the big red brocade curtains
To shut you in. Nor how the price for once
Was too high, and so much easier
Just to grab the nearest marble cherub
And bring the arm down, again and again
Until exhaustion.

Legendary Uncle Otto, whom they never knew,
Stretches the length of his apartment,
Fingers, toes still growing fast.
Soon he will reach across the city
And lie belly downwards from end to end of Europe.

Tattoo in the Convict Camp

At ten o'clock when the lights go down
And they know there'll be silence
Unless it's the dread expected, which is not to be
Thought of once between now and morning,
They turn to the little man cross-legged with his spine
Not fitting the wall and plead with him, 'Vlodya! Vlodya!
Show us the circus!' He laughs, and spits;
Touches their shoulders with the tips of his fingers
Before flicking open the buttons and belt and flies:
His bone-lean thighs are caparisoned horses
Leaping through hoops and back again;
Here shimmying up and down pectorals are the monkeys in fezes
Buttocks up to the audience and the pink tutus
Of the trapeze ballerinas bobbing right across
That diaphragm. Here are elephants
Docking their foreheads along a neural column:
They roll it like teak round and round their lips
Testing for flavour. And the lions on the biceps
Shake their manes and canines test for size
The head of the ringmaster popping out
Clean as a whistle to take his bow
From the spectators roaring now for the pièce
De résistance: cannon slowly tilting at the sky,
And a shiver going down them as their heads turn
Into the dome of the big top, hoping the shot
May go clear through the canvas and hit the immaculate stars.
They sigh 'Vlodya! Vlodya!' as he falls back sweating,
Is applauded and the spent circus animals rubbed down
To avoid the agues of fear and sequestration.
When they huddle back to cages, it's twenty degrees below.

The Prisoner of Katyn

'I have no interest now in what goes on outside:
After forty years you build your hell or palace
From the sticks they give you. I have only these
And they determine what manner of house I live in.
It is like this: always early morning,
And there are many pigs about me –
I was taking them to look for acorns in the wood.
I loved my pigs, had given each one a nickname,
Knew where each had a wart or strange knot in the hide
That you could put your thumb in like a fingerprint.
Some had just littered, and there was one of which
I was fondest, a small female, marbled black and gold.
That morning she ran just ahead of me, enjoying
The cool berries: it was the first time she had run free,
And she pushed at the dead leaves, the cold earth,
With her tiny snout. All around us the mists coiled
Like wood nymphs turning the trees to ghosts
With their long embraces; the hogs were centaurs
In an enchanted wood.

              And then, in ones and twos,
The cries started: through the pale O of the glades
This squealing of a stuck boar coming closer and closer
Till on all sides burst out of the silence running men,
Their mouths round and red as apples as they went down,
My pigs in a welter amongst them screaming and bolting
Into the executioners' rifles. When it was finished,
We heaved them together into the dug earth,
Watched their bodies curl like sticks of incense
In the milky air. Dead leaves were shovelled over
To make it new.

These were the last things that I saw outside;
Through these last windows I count each twig
And chart which way the first man blundered,
I recompose what kind of noise each man made when he died.
This is the house I walk in: it is always morning
And I am driving pigs into the spellbound wood.'

III

THE SHANGHAI OWNER OF THE BONSAI SHOP

Sent on a Mission to the Fruitlands of the South

Sent on a mission to the fruitlands of the south,
Leaving my sweet mistress, I had expected male friendship,
A comradely meal overlooking the cool autumn gardens.
Nothing prepared me for the woman turning with greeting
Outstretched and slight stoop towards me,
Nothing had warned of the ghost that flitted then over my face
Saying, This is what will be. Now as I toss this way
And that on my bed in the great city
All night I see this woman bowing and smiling,
Kissing the small of my back, whispering
'Lucky, lucky, to possess your soul'.

Blood Brothers

Someone somewhere in a winter landscape
Writes to a woman he has never seen
Asking how is her husband, dead for thirty years,
And having to send his letter by roundabout courier
As the country lies under siege
And many difficult borders are to be negotiated.

When the onions are sprouting, he is handed a reply:
It comes from a summer city in the south
Where yellow dust already chokes
Communications and men.
He reads of domestic squabbles, revered relatives
Who sloughed off wives for mistresses and wine,
Ministerial disgrace.
From the innermost roll uncurls a portrait:
His own hair, eyes, mouth, bone
In another's face, against another's backdrop
Of water and canals depicted
Measuring the unimagined
Painting himself in a discovered room.

This Morning the Postboy Brought Me a Letter

This morning the postboy brought me a letter
And we exchanged greetings, as we do often:
There was nothing out of the run of things
In what we said to each other; the morning was bright
And cold on the red leaves. As he walked away
Down the path, I noticed the characters
On what I was opening, that hand flew
Into my breast like a bird and I felt
My heart wings beat faster than the thrush
Caught in a snare. Then, as I leant on the porch,
Weak from desire, I also noticed how graceful
The step of the postboy was, how I had never seen
That he was light and delicate as a roebuck,
That the street where my house stands is paradise,
That a slip of paper may contain the whole of creation.

The Trail Is Not Obvious, Up Through the Blue Hills

The trail is not obvious, up through the blue hills:
Always difficulty with recalcitrant horses
And muleteers, excess luggage.
We pull gradually away from the city
And feel drunk with the new air.
Soon our voices drop to the silence;
Only the ack-ack of jackdaws and magpies
Rising out of the caves.

                The trees carpet our footsteps
In passing, up to the black mouth of pilgrimage
Where a child echoes over the valley.
We sit among the rocks like dwarves
And drink wine. We wait for stillness to come.

Often, Along the Road, He Sits Me in Winehouses

Often, along the road, he sits me in winehouses
And tells me to order anything I would like.
I fidget with the inlaid chopsticks,
The lacquered bowls, while he carouses
Behind a partition. Later, he is always solicitous,
Asking whether what I have tasted is good;
We tell each other of the strangely bent tree
Or the shadow over the river that we saw
Today journeying; there is always such a light
In his eye when he talks of where we will be together
Tomorrow. In these four months he has touched me
Only once, after too much wine, under a cold sun:
But his bent shoulders have blotted the world out.

I Waited on the Steps of Empire for the Woman I Loved

I waited on the steps of empire for the woman I loved.
Maybe quarter of an hour. The sun had never been warmer,
Nor the sky so free. I read a scroll, making a pretence
Of uninterest, watching the shoes
Of every woman who passed. Now, out of the corner
Of my mind's kingdom, she comes slowly, savouring
The day's heat, the multifariousness of the people,
While I, feigning blindness, see in this first glance
Her satin skin as it will be naked under my hands,
The taste of her lips when I give her a lover's token,
The sun careening at the top of heaven
Over our first embrace.

In the Library the Scholars Come and Go

In the library the scholars come and go:
Their thoughts and brushes make no sound.
All day they peruse pictures:
Whitened faces of ladies-in-waiting
Striking attitudes over a lute;
Turn, with the first frost, to depictions of horses,
Malevolent and strong-buttocked as their masters,
A steppe wind blurring manes and tails.

The brushes flick, interpret, annotate.

Outside, the leaves snap from the trees, unnoticed,
Settle, like pinpoints, dogs' eyes, in the dark
Where the indulgent and unchanging city turns:
In the streets, loud men play cards
And slap their fingers,
A woman tilts a frying pan,
And, at the village back, beside the rubbish pots,
A bride lets down her hair.

The Shanghai Owner of the Bonsai Shop

He keeps birds among his miniature gardens;
They hoop with condor wings around his paradise
Belling out their broken hearts. They are the philosophers'
Delicate meat, the harmony of their temples;
They leap from perch to perch till claws
Are scorched bare. Copper eats into the figs
And laurels, rouged, wrinkled
Before their time: they already know
All of torture and beauty and showing
Wisdom where it is not. The Shanghai owner
Of the bonsai shop is almost invisible
Behind the slats of his counting and annotating;
He hides the mistakes that return to him in a mountain mist.
There are days when he comes early and sits
Behind the unlit screens painted with courtesans;
Over the eyes slit with desire he pulls down
The shutters; and at the back of his shop
The lark-throated women sing in ecstasy
Under his long fingers.

Don't. When We Go Upstairs

Don't. When we go upstairs
To the hired room, don't stint your hands.
Don't spare your mercies.
Lie down beside me and let my fingers
Unfold the book of your face, the scroll
Of your body. We shall decipher the meaning
Of our most intimate characters, learn
To tell all the processes of touch.
When we go upstairs to the hired room,
Don't begrudge kisses: your tongue
Undoes the box where my soul sings.

I, Who Had Accounted Myself a Connoisseur of Love

I, who had accounted myself a connoisseur of love,
From smallest trifles to the edge of madness,
Had never yet known this: the loved one standing
In a common room, smiling, smiling through the throng
Of people, and I myself in full flow of wit
Laughing with my back turned to her; the whole
World with its hubbub no louder in our fainting minds
Than one bird singing out of season, the echo
Of our own cries in the night.

Here in the Water Gardens I Am to Meet Him

Here in the water gardens I am to meet him –
I watch the bronze and metal plumage of the winter geese
Arc and arc over the water; their high longing
Cries sting my heart. Their necks are sinewy
As my lover's, their breast as deep.
I lean over the bridge, watch the water break
Beneath wings as they drop out of the leaden air.
How will it be when we have grown tired
Of each other, your eye that encompasses the world
Turning dead towards me?

Meeting After a Journey

When you sit again at my table
Your hair has changed. The last time I saw you
It was blue as raven's plumage.
Now I see the silvering of age.
As I pour wine, you tell me of your successes,
Promotion, how you are much sought after
Even by those who rule. I congratulate,
Remind you how we stayed up all night
As students, talking over only tea and onions
When your hair was blue. You laugh,
Stretch out your hand towards me;
Together we pull back the curtains
And watch the trees bend in the moon.

Grandfather's Winter Coat Hangs on the Wall

Grandfather's winter coat hangs on the wall,
Become a decoration; foreigners' hands admire the inner fur,
Its outward elegance: they do not notice the savage smell of civet
Nor the bloodstain down in the corner,
Spilt a certain autumn afternoon when he tripped
Running to tell his general of civil disobedience
And had to write despatches all night with bloody fingers
Before the battle; how he used it as covering
On the forced marches and as packaging
For exquisite boneware over the mountain passes
Till they reached the sea.

In this new place there are no winters
And all the old words fall into disuse.
During the day we practise our new voices;
Under the palm's big shadow a grandchild tries the snowcoat on.

Two Men Met on a Road

Two men met on a road
And said, suppose the horses had needed
Changing sooner, or I had not been thirsty;
It had been cooler or we had come closer
To the next large town? Then they bent and washed
Their faces, shoulders in the nearby brook,
Shared fruit and wine resting in the shade
Of the willow trees, saying, suppose we had
Not known each other then, and you had kept her,
Or I had never seen her laughing grace;
We neither had watched her naked in the moon?
Down at the river's edge the churned earth retains
A while the press of hooves, feet side by side,
Toes touching by the running water.

IV

FIRST SNOW

First Snow

The water was always there, behind the houses:
On busy days, the city grew masts
Above shopkeepers and sailors tossing
Words from different ends of the earth.
Their goods smelt of tar, a foreigner's skin
Like the yellow man who'd given her a ribbon
In the pub's shadow and chucked her with slim fingers
Under the chin.

Daily the gates of the outside world opened
And shut to let the travellers in:
She swung on the hinges above them,
Appropriating cargoes big as suns
To glow behind cupboards, under the bed
Until morning.

Except that one morning, when, having to run for bread
Down the foul stairway, least thinking of hot silk
Or glossy-skinned men, she pushed the door
Onto a world where no stain nor jagged edge
Remained, anointed with so much white
That she could hardly see
How the ordinary air was thick with crystals,
Each narrow street decked with shreds of paradise.

The Ewe

My mother sits by this stream
All of twenty-five years ago,
Her war-time heavy-duty swimsuit
Tied at the back and giving round
Egg-shaped stomach and breasts;
She watches the water.

        We picnicked that day
Driven mad by gnats and having to spread
Napkins over the oozing peat bank;
There were rank boiled eggs, tinned salmon
Sandwiches, dandelion and burdock pop.
We had watched the golfers placing
Their shots between ram and ewe
And down in the chapel of Kareol.

My mother sat on the river bank
Watching the weeds bright as emeralds
Fronding the stones; the cold grasping
Our ankles when we stepped in made us cry.
'Don't drink,' she said, 'though this water
Is clear as silk, don't drink.'

I turned over the stones very carefully,
Not wishing too much to discover something
Unpleasant, yet curious for the icy stream-bed
And hoping most of all for a glimpse of life,
Of silver, battling up into the pools.
My arms and shoulders burned; toes no
Longer a part of me – 'don't drink'
She kept calling, and my father oiled her back
Under the stunted hawthorn.

We found it upstream, a big fleck of white
At first, taking its ease by the riverside
But too still. Horns lying against
The tree trunk, a sallow yellow, and the
Long nose rind sticking out of the wool.
And so much of it! Cream and ginger and
Saffron turned muddy from dog sniff
And sluicing of rain; a dried belly
In the sun.

                Why had she been surprised
Here beside water that should take off
Thirst? Had she hung her head low
Over the babbling current to listen,
Or merely, fighting the pain inside,
Gazed with veiled eyes at the endless
Movement away from her, the sound
Of time's slippage?

I waded almost till dusk that patch
Of river, searching for worlds
Beneath the broken water, the shape
Of secrets under the make-believe growth.
And I hear from the bank my mother
Calling out of the deepening shadow,
'Tread carefully. Hold onto the branches.
Don't drink that water. Don't fall.'

Norman Terrace

In my mind's eye we still sit
In the dark together, you on the edge
Of my bed. The car beams trail down
The ceiling like spectres;
You tell of the phantom trucks pulling
Their slag up the red-hot hillside
As if they still did.

But now it is I who sit upright
Smoothing the bedclothes, hearing
Your small voice come from beyond the light.
We have forgotten the carts spilling
Their load like blood over the mountain.
Tonight we have only the dark
In which you lie listening for voices I
Never heard, conjuring all the years
When I never was into this room.

You curl on your side, saying, 'Why?
Why, when he knew that I'd help him?'
And I, having no answer for these night-time
Fears, hold your fingers, turning them over
And over like the waves your dead brother,
Remembering how you would sit through the hours
With me, delighting also in the car beams
Tracing their fingers pitilessly down our lives
Like ghosts.

Fulbeck, 1944

(for my father)

Parade ground, under the wide eye
Of the airborne mind a cross of cardboard
Puckered at the edge by cowslip, sassafras,
Toy knights and airmen turning in the appointed place:
Only for one more hour routine configurations
Of call-tower, windsock, dip, bank, ground go-ahead;
Then, the rattling past farms, the buttercup dykes running to the sea!

Parade ground, big as a desert
To the men drilling between wingtip and wingtip
Among the silent mechanisms moving
With instinctive logic to where the player will drop his hand,
Miscalculate, and strew his pieces
In a ball of blood and metal and burning leather
Across the disfigured board.

Over the square come the phalanxes, running:
Pawns to aid pawns, and the navigator
Who lately dreamt of new-mown grass, his girl's full breasts,
Cradles more tenderly the dying man he fears
Than ever any beloved; and tonight instead will lie
Awake and try and try again to make the fabric
Of his life seal up rent garments, tattered face,
And roll away the eclipse at noon.

Beachy Head

I see you now, my mother and father,
Coming up this cliff slowly, though you did
So but yesterday, as if you are long dead.
Here my father, placing his legs askew
As he pulls for breath, turns to look back
Down the twisting path they have come.
My mother touches her arthritic knee.
And all around, the great arc of the world
Encloses them. O keep back from the dazzling edge,
Daddy, don't move with your vertigo closer
To the drop, the terrible slippage.
Lay out your provisions and go giddy
With the clouds running overhead.
And my mother unwraps the boiled eggs,
Lets tea from the thermos, lies down close
To the ticking grass while across to France
The years flash back and forth
With their insistent whisper, hish, hish,
Lullaby, wash away our hurt down the shingle;
How these two rheumaticky people shimmer
Like gods in the grass.

In Memoriam D.L. Davies (1926-1976)

I ask whether pyjamas, toothbrush,
Underpants of the man who now moves
Inattentively from room to room, scarcely noticing
His only daughter who packs necessities
Into a suitcase, like a mother sending a son
On a new journey and shedding the occasional,
Surreptitious tear, except that here
Any tears that will be shed are not from fear
Of what has still to come; instead of what must now
Forever be, not the mother consoling her son,
But a father without a brother, capriciously
Wading into the sea and going waste.
We drive into a storm: a big red sun,
Washed behind rain clouds, shows the day is done.
We telephone, and eat, are washed abed
By the night's great tide over the careless dead.

Nocturnal Conversation

(for Laurence Davies)

Four in the morning, rolled in the sour smell of my husband's limbs,
And already the steel crust of dawn widening over the housetops:
My arm uncurls towards the telephone in strange slow motion
As if no longer joined to me; nor does surprise come
When down the bad line drops that voice last heard
In gaiety across a summer table, or flung by the sea wind,
A scarf ravelling itself around my head.

The darkness makes us gentle: barely present are the other
     conversations,
Hysteria, pleading relatives, mistrust.
Only the learning of new hopes, and then dependencies,
Remains; how through the shuttered afternoons
Your hands, like voices, on the keys
Relayed a world of order satisfied;
The close-meshed net denying
Every flawed thing.
                  Fear made you stumble,
Slam the piano lid down each time,
Each time a severed conversation.

Now there is truce between us: your words
Possess this room, the furniture
That stocks my head with daubed, stained, splintered edges
I try to piece into a lacquered chair.
This I meant to tell you long ago –
                  but when I speak
Your voice hazes. Our line cracks dead.

Dawn has come; my husband's arm,
Flung to retrieve me into sleep,
Shows white across the blanket.
The sour scent of his living touches me.
I lie, listening to the traffic wake along the streets;
How it carries with it the sudden presence
Of your mute suicide.

V

ASCENSION

Incident

This body is real. Under the dust sheets
It accumulates decay. We never thought
In this quiet place to find a horror –
A corpse laid out. I could touch the gauze
Masking torture. His face is wrenched sideways,
The collar bones have cracked.
Above the cars run all ways with insouciance.
Women exchange the price of cabbages;
Police idle on corners. Maybe the disaffected,
Nevertheless, out of fear to see this on the refuse tip,
Gave a place, temporarily, where he could be
Locked out of sight.

His mother and the women who knew him
Petitioned the authorities; they sat up
Until late in the night speculating
But the body was never found.
Then circumstances changed: stock markets faltered,
There was redeployment of forces, new government.
And he stayed down here all the while.

When we came, he'd been in the cellar too long
To smell; the awkward angles of dislocation
Are rigid, bones stick through the skin.
From the right one woman for ever rushes
Towards him, gesturing: look. Look. This
Is real. Such intimacy takes us unawares.
The clay, the blood are real, the easy
Forgetting in a corner, this woman's dry acquaintance
With grief.
               Breathing sharper air,
We reverse away down branch-strewn avenues:
In the taverns we drink his blood,
Roll bread down into crumbs.

This Was a High Time in My Life

This was a high time in my life:
A time of blue and gold
When rain was soft about my head
Heaven in my hold.

Before the rocks and shallows came
The sudden deeps and snares
Where only faith keeps my keel
From splintering unawares.

When I Was Felled to the Ground

When I was felled to the ground
By a word, and wriggled like a
Worm, spitting out my grief;
When I felt the heel of desire
Hot on my neck, and knew it was this
So mastered me

Then I saw an angel standing
Between the bookshelves
Carrying in his hand a fiery broadsword
I recognised all the orchard
That lay beyond him;
I understood.

How Long Before I Put You

How long before I put you,
My God, first among men?
The light slants on the bed
Where pale and beautiful Guilt
Lies sleeping.

Soon he will wake and genuinely
Cry and open the window
For fresh air, He will set about
Extinguishing himself.

Ah! but his desire to live
Is strong, very strong.
When he comes knocking on my door
Begging for food, of course
I'll invite him into my bed
And warm with my breasts
His starved limbs.

Let Me Go, God

Let me go, God.
These walls hem me in.
My blood's a tracery
That would lovingly wind itself
In a warp of sin.

Open the door, God,
Out of this house.
The cruel windows bring
All that's desirable
To desire's spouse.

Let me go, God.
The streets are bright and wide.
Into this poorhouse
The heat of possession
Runs its tide.

But when I come to your door, God,
Will you have me in?
Open wide the door, Lord:
Your blood alone's the tracery
That winds us lovingly
Out of sin.

It's Not Suffering, It's Not

It's not suffering, it's not
The passionate resentment of incapacity,
The curtains in the sick man's room;
Nor jealousy, betrayal's clean stab,
Nor a train departing from the stage
For ever. Not yet the sudden fall
Of destiny, police or angels standing
At the door; a son buying a one-way ticket
Or the quick, heady intervals of war.

No, this is a window tapping, a creaking chair;
The mind busy rooting in the stink
Of its own dung, or soul with trowel in hand
Measuring up the gaol bars for its self's
Entombment. It's nothingness, the absence
Of all pain or joy or ability to hold the world
In the slight grasses of a minute; it's the moment
Passing without care. Denial, accidie:
The open mouth, slow hand and slow indifference:
Suffering's child, suffering's dead noon.

I Heard Children Laughing

I heard children laughing
Out of sight. A moment before
Silence, and now this sound
Like larks rising over the fields.
And as I listened, this laughter
Swelled with something different,
Going out of it the apples
In the first orchard, a darkness
Entering in till soon it was
A noise I could scarcely bear to hear,
Full of Babel and quarrels and grief.
Then the children were all called
Inside, out of my sight, their cries
Slipping away as if into an endless
Tunnel, and there was only one child
Left, shut out by a chance slamming
Of the door, raging at destiny.

When I Woke, I Was in this Factory

'When I woke, I was in this factory,
Many people working like demons
Along the dank halls. Rope turning
Down the long galleries, or putting rivets
In things on the production line, though
I couldn't see what. And the din
Remarkable for its groans and sighs
And Ahs, not all unpleasurable,
And muffled squeaks in corners.
Sometimes the light came in great beams
Through the soaring windows, so you could
See all the motes and how they danced
Tremulously like halos turning the white
Skin of the girls to barley.
There seemed to be no stopping all
That went on here, day and night
This threshing of movement, the squeals,
Sudden sleepy eyes.

           Then there was difference,
Slowing, agitation, for it was the day
Of payment. All the machines stopped.
The great paymaster swaggered through the door.
Girls wiped their hands down their dresses
And adjusted themselves; the men looked
Melancholy. Each one, I noticed,
With the same compulsion to tear wide
His envelope, and weep. Down the long
Rope galleries, coming closer and closer
To my turn, how the women looked beautiful!
How milk-blue their breasts, and how they
Smelled of grass! So I lingered in the
Side aisles longer and longer, and kissed
And mounted them under the benches, made
Promises to meet in the garden
In the cool of the day, until no longer
Could I postpone my pay-check. Why

This sudden fear when I look into
The eyes of the paymaster, his handsome
Retainers? I tear wide my envelope
Wherein I find written the word: Death.'

Ascension

Not having celebrated, nor even thought
Of this great day, but set upon a road
Preoccupied with the weight of matter bought,
Slow growth of life's vine about my throat,
I pass, and gradually see, the wheat in sail,
Trees silk with blossom throwing on my shore
Unmindful beauty. Alone on this highway
I move, seem fretful, casting out for more;
And then it comes, the suddenly remembered thing:
Out of copses, hollows, the earth's breast,
Loud, bright as water, opening white-hot wings
That change this strip of tarmac into heaven's resin,
These farms, cream-flowered hawthorns, cattle dressed
All for redemption, stripped of sin.